100

THINGS TO DO IN
DALLAS
FORT WORTH
BEFORE YOU
DIE

D0012534

100

THINGS TO DO IN
DALLAS
FORT WORTH
BEFORE YOU
DIE

SALLY BLANTON ★ ANDREA ALCORN
STEVE RICHARDSON

REEDY PRESS
St. Louis, Missouri

This book is dedicated to you:
for your passion,
living life to the fullest,
and celebrating memory-making,
rich experiences!

Dallas is

"... a city that has the most entrepreneurial people in the world."
—Linda Ivy (Socialite, Philanthropist)

"... a city filled with kind, generous, hospitable people. We are changing and maturing as a city, especially in the science and technology fields."
—Dr. Irene Willingham (Neurological Surgeon)

"... becoming one of the largest trendiest fashion cities in the world."
—Prashi Shah (Fashion Designer)

"... a vibrant, diverse urban environment."
—Jon Beasley (President of the Turtle Creek Association)

"... exciting, and building for a better tomorrow."
—Carol Aaron (Philanthropist)

"... a great town with some of the best live theatre in the country."
—Terry Martin (Artistic Director, WaterTower Theatre)

"... absolutely the best place to live and raise a family."
—Nancy Berry (Speaker/Author)

"... a great city with spirit and amazing philanthropy."
—Joyce Pickering (Executive Director, Shelton School)

"... a city with a heart."
—Janelle Friedman (CFO, Friedman & Feiger Attorneys at Law)

"... a world class city with many great people and lots of sunshine."
—Lynn Dealey (Artist/Illustrator)

"... becoming a cultural giant."
—Darlene Cass (Civic Leader)

Fort Worth is

". . . one of the friendliest cities in the country. If you want to see Texas, then you come to Fort Worth."
—Tim Love (Celebrity Chef, Lonesome Dove Restaurant)

". . . moos and sonic booms! Ospreys, F35s, and longhorns on hoof. It is the biggest little town where heritage and the future know no bounds. Fort Worth, I luv yew!"
—Hap Baggett (CEO, HB Properties)

". . . a city of authentic givers. They ask, 'When?' and 'How much can I do to help?'"
—Olivia Kearney (Philanthropist)

". . . a legendary city of contrast, culture, and cowboys. A city of fine arts and fine people."
—Mary Shannon

Copyright © 2014 by Reedy Press, LLC

Reedy Press
PO Box 5131
St. Louis, MO 63139, USA
www.reedypress.com

No part of this publication may be reproduced or transmitted in any form or by any means, electronic or mechanical, including photocopy, recording, or any information storage and retrieval system, without permission in writing from the publisher.

Permissions may be sought directly from Reedy Press at the above mailing address or via our website at www.reedypress.com.

Library of Congress Control Number: 2014932740

ISBN: 978-1-935806-57-8

Design by Jill Halpin

Printed in the United States of America
14 15 16 17 18   5 4 3 2

Please note that websites, phone numbers, addresses, and company names are subject to change or cancellation. We did our best to relay the most accurate information available, but due to circumstances beyond our control, please do not hold us liable for misinformation. When exploring new destinations, please do your homework before you go.

For more information, upcoming author events, and booksignings, please visit us on Facebook at 100 Things To Do In Dallas/Fort Worth Before You Die.

CONTENTS

xii

PREFACE

Why does the "Metroplex" draw thirteen million visitors here each year? What is it about this flourishing epicenter, midway between two coasts, which claims such high praise from around the globe? One answer would be the truth of Dallas's slogan: "Big Things Happen Here" . . . and do they ever!

DFW is bold and bodacious, synonymous with "the art of the deal," incredible architecture, a state-of-the-art cultural district, "America's Team," deep-pocketed philanthropists, and ever so much more. This economic and cultural hub has all the elements that make up the nation's fastest growing economy: banking, oil and gas, real estate, fashion, culture, professional and collegiate sports, technology, major universities, a presidential library, and a plethora of entertaining attractions and events that contribute to the high-energy, can-do spirit.

The sprawling Metroplex covers twelve counties and more than 9,250 square miles—larger than the states of New Jersey, Connecticut, Delaware, and Rhode Island. Now that's big. DFW also offers big opportunities; big sports; big fancy cars; big expensive mansions; big skies; big museums; big nationally renowned chefs; big-time entrepreneurs; big business; big steaks; big times; and, most important, big experiences.

With our combined 125 years of working and playing in the Metroplex, we're sharing some of our secrets and favorite experiences of this vibrant area. *100 Things to Do in Dallas–Fort Worth Before You Die* will not take you on a tour, join you in a Texas brawl over what is the biggest or the best, or brag that we could include *every* secret and *every* noble experience to be had in these parts. Life is simply too short for all of that, and this is not a guidebook. Since the Metroplex is ever-growing and ever-changing, we focused on the selections that were not only uniquely Dallas–Fort Worth, but have also stood the test of time.

A basic truth of life is that it ends, and our experiences help define us when we're gone. We have tried to fill this little book with potential experiences that make life worth living. With the advent of social media and phones that act as computers, we are constantly on the go—so busy doing, we forget to be living. As Tim McGraw reminds us in his award-winning song, "live like you are dying." Life really is for living.

It has been a joy searching the corners and pockets of these great cities. Whether you were born in DFW, just moved here, or are just visiting, there are more options than ever: museums, high-fashion centers, parks, lakes, tours, fabulous restaurants, glamorous hotels, cultural events, festivals, attractions, events, and on. So strap on your boots and go full-tilt into what the Metroplex has to offer. And we hope you will have a Texas-sized time making memories.

100

THINGS TO DO IN
DALLAS
FORT WORTH
BEFORE YOU
DIE

CROSS OVER
THE ICONIC
MARGARET HUNT HILL BRIDGE

Dallas has an answer to San Francisco's Golden Gate Bridge. Eminent designer Santiago Calatrava's six-lane suspension bridge across the Trinity River is the first vehicular bridge of its kind in the United States. Named after the late Dallas oil heiress and civic leader, the bridge's signature feature is a gleaming 400-foot white arch. Nearly twelve million pounds of structural steel was used in the construction. An explosion of growth also has occurred near one of the bases of the bridge. The Trinity Groves area is a fifteen-acre restaurant, retail, artist, and entertainment destination fostering startup concepts and businesses. Trinity Groves is called "the home of fresh, new concepts."

N. Riverfront Blvd., Dallas • 214-671-9500 • www.strinitygroves.com

PAY HOMAGE TO PEGASUS
AT THE MAGNOLIA HOTEL DALLAS

According to its current owners, the Magnolia Hotel Dallas was the tallest building west of the Mississippi River when it opened for business in 1922. It also was one of the first high-rises in the country with air conditioning. The red neon Pegasus, the Winged Victory symbol of Big D, shines brightly at the top of the twenty-nine-story boutique hotel. The horse is bigger than it looks, weighing fifteen tons! The Magnolia Hotel Dallas, in earlier days the headquarters of the Magnolia Petroleum Co., treats guests royally with extras such as evening wine and beer, bedtime cookie buffet, and gratis hot breakfast for two. It features a hip lobby and clubroom. Great restaurants are in easy walking distance. Neiman Marcus is next door, so happy shopping.

1401 Commerce St., Dallas • 214-915-6500 • www.magnoliahotels.com

HAVE AN ADULT BEVERAGE
AT THE ROSEWOOD MANSION BAR

The Rosewood Mansion Bar and Hotel is dark, romantic, and reminiscent of the glamorous 1940s. If only those Mansion walls could talk. Major deals are closed and marriage proposals are made. Patrons enjoy dancing, fine dining, and celebrations of all sorts. An intimate bar is inside the lovely Rosewood Mansion Hotel on Turtle Creek, which is known for service and amenities to please the most discriminating guests. The Mansion was built in 1908 by cotton baron Sheppard King. A large, lovely patio is a great place for meeting friends. Turtle Creek is one of the most beautiful districts, known for its luxury high-rises and lush, meandering creek.

2821 Turtle Creek Blvd., Dallas • 214-559-2100
www.rosewoodhotels.com

For a touch of European elegance, go to the Adolphus Hotel downtown for a "spot 'o tea." Some guests who have preceded you there are Queen Elizabeth II, the Vanderbilts, and Oscar de la Renta. 1321 Commerce St., Dallas, 214-742-8200
www.hoteladolphus.com

Tip:

Continue your museum touring by visiting the Meadows Museum on the SMU campus. Algur H. Meadows began collecting Spanish art in the 1950s. The majority of the collection focuses on the Spanish "Golden Age." There are masterworks by Velazquez, Goya, Murillo, and Ribera. Modern works include Picasso and Gris. Free on Thursdays after 5:00. Closed on Mondays.

Meadows Museum:
5900 Bishop Blvd., 214-768-1688
www.meadowsmuseumdallas.org

HAIL TO THE CHIEF
AT THE GEORGE W. BUSH
PRESIDENTIAL LIBRARY AND MUSEUM

Lucky Dallas! We were chosen by the Bush family to be the home of the forty-third president's library. Visitors enter the museum, adjacent to the SMU campus, through six acres of native prairie grasses and wild flowers. The building's architecture is splendid with its clean modern lines. Guests are enchanted by an array of treasured gifts from heads of state on display in Freedom Hall. The enormous wrap-around video overhead seems three-dimensional. The replica of the "Oval Office" is accurate to the last detail. The 9-11 artifacts, especially the twisted girders from the World Trade Center, make a powerful statement. There are interactive exhibits and lots of memorabilia. Try the excellent "43 Restaurant." Chef John Maas is in the kitchen preparing some of the Bush family favorites for your enjoyment. Texans have bragging rights to *three* presidential libraries. "We train 'em in Texas, then send 'em on to lead the free world."

2943 SMU Blvd., Dallas • 214-346-1557
www.georgewbushlibrary.smu.edu

FALL IN LOVE
WITH TEX-MEX FIRSTS

The Metroplex is home to several Tex-Mex inventions, and your visit is incomplete without experiencing the global revolution of this cuisine. Characteristic of the borders of Texas and Mexico, Tex-Mex is known for its heavy use of cheese, beans, spices, pork, and beef. The oldest family-owned Mexican restaurant in town is Tupinamba's, owned by the Dominguez family. This family introduced Dallas to nachos and the sour cream enchilada. Ask for the daily-made hot sauce. It's not on the menu, but it will make you say *Arriba*!

Your Tex-Mex adventure will not be complete unless you try a frozen margarita. Did you know the world's first frozen margarita machine was created in Dallas by Mariano Martinez? Though the machine now resides in the Smithsonian's National Museum of American History, it's still worth it to imbibe one of these famed frozen libations at Mariano's La Hacienda Ranch.

Tupinamba's

12270 Inwood Rd., Dallas, 972-991-8148
www.tupinambarestaurant.com

La Hacienda Ranch

(multiple locations) 173900 Preston Road, #100, Dallas
972-248-2424, www.laharanch.com

Mi Cocina (multiple locations)

11661 Preston Rd., Dallas, 214-265-7704
www.micocinarestaurants.com

Mr. Mesero

4444 McKinney Ave., Dallas, 214-780-1991
www.mrmesero.com

Joe T. Garcia's Mexican Restaurant

2201 N. Commerce St., Fort Worth, 817-626-4356
www.joets.com

Ojeda's Mexican Restaurant

4617 Maple Ave., Dallas, 214-528-8383
www.ojedasdallas.com

El Fenix (over 18 locations in Dallas/Fort Worth)

6811 W. Northwest Highway, Dallas, 214-363-5279
www.elfenix.com

E-Bar Tex Mex

1901 N. Haskell Ave., Dallas, 214-824-3227
www.ebartexmex.com

Mattito's (multiple locations)

7778 Forest Lane, Dallas, 214-377-9576
www.mattitos.com

BUY PREVIOUSLY LOVED BOOKS AND MUSIC
AT THE FLAGSHIP HALF PRICE BOOKS

This is the "mother ship"—the corporate headquarters of a little shop that started in a Dallas laundromat in 1972. The company, which has grown to more than one hundred stores in sixteen states, buys and sells almost anything except yesterday's newspaper. There is something pretty special about buying a stranger's book. You might just find some interesting notes jotted in the margins. This store is a book lover's wonderland. Vinyl record purists will have a field day here as well. Wander to your heart's content. There is a quaint café for your reading or Wi-Fi pleasure. A helpful staff person is always nearby. Audio books, video games, movies, children's books, and new, unique items are also featured. One customer said, "I want to live here. Literally pay rent and live."

5803 Northwest Highway, Dallas • 214-379-8000 • www.hpb.com

HEAR A FIERY SERMON
BY T.D. JAKES AT POTTER'S HOUSE

There are 30,000 members and fifty outreach ministries at the famed Potter's House. Pastor Jakes has written more than thirty books, several on the *New York Times* best-seller list. Pastor Jakes broadcasts to countless listeners. This mega evangelistic church is non-denominational. The annual MegaFest draws more than 75,000 people. (T. D. Jakes accompanied President George W. Bush to visit the Katrina victims.)

6777 W. Kiest Blvd., Dallas ● 800-BISHOP2 ● www.thepottershouse.org
1707 San Jacinto St., Dallas ● 214-969-0111 ● www.firstdallas.org
2215 Ross Ave., Dallas ● 214-871-1362 ● www.cathedralguadalupe.org

The First Dallas Baptist Church downtown has completed a multimillion-dollar expansion. Founded in 1868, the expanded campus is a huge spiritual beacon in downtown. The grand, ornate fountain, with its sixty-eight-foot cross, contributes to the majesty of the worship facility. The Cathedral Santuario de Guadelupe is a rare historic gem that is a fine example of High Victorian Gothic Architecture. It has 25,000 registered families, making it one of the largest Catholic congregations in America.

MOSEY ON OVER
TO COWTOWN

Downtown Fort Worth is a very pedestrian-friendly place. Sundance Square is thirty-five historic blocks where people safely play, work, and live. The focal point is the Nancy Lee and Perry Bass Performance Hall, named one of the ten best opera houses in the nation. Other attractions are the Hyenna's Comedy Club inside Lone Star, which hosts live music several times a week, Circle Theatre, Jubilee Theatre, Scat Jazz Lounge, and the Sid Richardson Museum. The Mercury Chophouse has a wonderful patio with live music. The 8.0 can seat you in an inviting outdoor pavilion. Parking in Sundance is free all day on weekends and on weekdays after 5 p.m.

Main Street, Fort Worth • 817-255-5700 • www.sundancesquare.com

Tip:

Push pedals with your friends at
a COWTOWN CYCLE PARTY.
Who thought of this great idea? The Cycle
Party is powered entirely by groups up to
fifteen people; the group effort propels the
bus-like vehicle. It is a BYOB system and has
a killer sound system for tunes. Perfect for
sightseeing, parties, and team-building. Groups
are provided a driver for a two-hour tour.
682-42-CYCLE

SING "THE STAR SPANGLED BANNER"
AT GLOBE LIFE BALLPARK
IN ARLINGTON

A few years back the Texas Rangers were the fourth franchise in the DFW area in terms of popularity behind the Cowboys, Mavericks, and Stars. That all changed with back-to-back trips to the World Series in 2010 and 2011. The Rangers have now drawn 3 million fans multiple times in their home park, which has been recently renovated and updated. When games aren't being played, tours start at the First Base Box Office on the south side of the stadium where there is a "Tour Window." Treat yourself to a Boomstick, a one-pound, twenty-four-inch hot dog topped with sautéed onions, chili, and cheese. Collect a souvenir at the Majestic Grand Slam Shop located in center field.

1000 Ballpark Way, Arlington • 817-273-5222 (game tickets)
817-273-5099 (tours) • www.texasrangers.com

WEAR BLACK LEATHER
TO STROKERS

This place is the real deal, and one of the largest in the country. On a nice Sunday there could be 1,000 or 2,000 bikes on Strokers' several acres. It's "Blues, Burgers, and Bikes," and you'll see gleaming chrome, leather chaps, boots, halter tops, and do-rags galore. If you don't ride a Harley or a custom cruiser, you will still be welcome to enjoy this sub-culture experience. And yes, you will see the infamous, yet well-behaved, Bandidos and Scorpions gang members mingling with the young professionals and the more elite biker boys and babes. The roar of the engines is deafening, but in a good way. Be sure to check out the apparel for sale and displays of super cool custom bikes. Rick Fairless, owner, has had two of his own reality shows, and is known for building the highest quality custom bikes in the world.

9304 Harry Hines Blvd., Dallas ● 214-357-0707 ● www.strokersdallas.com

Tip:

For the ultimate in pampering your "spoiled self," schedule a treatment session at one of these spas that continue to receive high marks: Hiatus Spa, Massage Envy, Facelogic, King Spa & Sauna, Grand Spa International, Spa at the Rosewood Crescent Hotel, Serenity Spa at the Ritz Carlton, ZaSpa at Hotel Za Za, Exhale Spa at Hotel Palomar, Pure Spa and Salon, Spa at Cooper Institute, or Mokara Spa at the Omni Fort Worth Hotel.

INDULGE YOURSELF
AT THE SPA CASTLE URBAN RESORT

Escape from the ordinary at a magnificent, mansion-like facility offering a complete Asian spa experience, beautiful outdoor pool, savory cuisine, bar, and luxury hotel. The three-story spa defies description, but the outstanding features are the spacious design and the pristine cleanliness. "Sauna Valley" features ten ornate rooms, each with a different type of experience. The outdoor spa pools offer lots of choices, or you can just laze the afternoon away in a rented cabana. Indulging in treatments will add additional fees. The cover charge is $35, which includes access to many delights. Small kids price is $20. It's right off of George Bush Freeway.

1020 Raiford Rd., Carrollton ● 972-446-6800 ● www.spacastleusa.com

WING IT
TO THE FABULOUS FRONTIERS OF FLIGHT OR THE CAVANAUGH FLIGHT MUSEUMS

Experience the stories of those who went "higher, faster, farther and first" in aviation, space, and flight history. You will be impressed from the moment you enter the 100,000-square-foot facility near Love Field. What a great venue for exploring the history and progress of aviation! See the Apollo 7 Space Capsule, which traveled 4.5 million miles, on loan from the Smithsonian. How about a Southwest Airlines Gallery that is anchored by a real 737? Kids' programs are presented during the summer. At Cavanaugh's Flight Museum in Addison, catch a ride on a historic aircraft, such as a Warbird, or book a helicopter tour. The majority of the planes in the collection are airworthy. There are many vintage cars and armored vehicles displayed. Air shows for special events originate here.

6911 Lemmon Ave., Dallas • 214-350-3600 • www.flightmuseum.com
4572 Claire Chennault St., Addison • 972-380-8800
www.cavanaughflightmuseum.com

HAVE AN UNPARALLELED EXPERIENCE
AT THE LEGENDARY TEXAS–OU GAME

Soak up the exciting atmosphere of two classic rivalries at the Cotton Bowl Stadium each fall. Since 1929, Texas and Oklahoma have met on the field during the Texas State Fair. Cotton Bowl Stadium, which now seats more than 90,000 fans, has hosted most of those games with Burnt Orange (Texas) fans occupying half the seats, Crimson and Cream (OU) fans the other. Getting a seat to this game is like trying to get an audience with the Pope. The scalper's route is usually the only way to go. Regardless, on the second Saturday in October it's fun to watch the fans at the State Fair even if you are just walking the midway.

Also at the Cotton Bowl: a Southwestern Athletic Conference game between Grambling State and Prairie View A&M is usually played on the previous Saturday. The highlight is the halftime "Battle of the Bands" between the high-steeping musicians from the two historically African American institutions that have played here since the mid-1980s.

Cotton Bowl Stadium: 3921 Martin Luther King Jr. Blvd., Fair Park, Dallas, 972-263-8374 • www.bigtex.com

BRING IN THE NEW YEAR
AT VICTORY PARK PLAZA

Rivaling Times Square, Big D's NYE Party is growing each year. It takes about 400 staff and crew members to produce the celebration. Multiple hi-def cameras, two music stages, gigantic HD screens, celebrity guests, plus one of the largest New Year's fireworks displays in the nation make this a memorable way to end and begin a year. Parking can be challenging, so think about DART Rail and Trinity Railway Express, which run to Victory Station at the American Airlines Center. Sing "Auld Lang Syne" in a silly party hat. Bliss Spa at the W Dallas Victory Hotel, nearby, is ideal for a New Year's Eve recovery treatment.

2013 Victory Park Lane, Dallas
www.victorypark.com, www.wdallasvictory.com

KICK BACK FOR A WHILE
AT KLYDE WARREN PARK

A lush park downtown! Free to the public, as parks should be. Chill out or enjoy food trucks, yoga, park boot camp, zumba, music performances, free WiFi, and a playground. All this, plus your furry friends are welcome. Savor Restaurant and Lark on the Park, with its great patio, are popular dining establishments. You can host your own event at the park, even a wedding. Check out the twenty-minute Skyline Tour, where a guide will point out significant architectural highlights in various skyscrapers. The park is named for the son of Kelcy Warren, Texas-rich energy executive, with an estimated wealth of several billion.

2012 Woodall Rodgers Freeway, Dallas • 214-716-4500
www.klydewarrenpark.org

A parking garage is across the street, but if you catch a trolley to the park on McKinney Avenue . . . voilà, no searching for a parking space.

SPICE UP YOUR LIFE
WITH ALL THINGS TEXAN

Many come to Dallas and Fort Worth searching for a real cowboy. Though most "Big Texans" have moved on down the trail, the unique culinary style of authentic Texas ingredients and the flavor of ranch days gone by is still vibrant in the area. For a true Texas experience, forget your weight watcher diet and channel your urban cowboy with a juicy chicken-fried steak with jalapeno cream gravy, a butter-brushed flat iron steak, or a favorite from a nearby ranch. You can certainly round 'em up at the Ranch at Las Colinas because it doesn't get more Texan. Wash down that Bob White Quail and Wild Boar with a Dublin, Texas Dr. Pepper. "Made in Texas By Texans," Stampede 66's Stephan Pyles cooks up Texas Classics. Try the Honey-Fried Chicken served with Mashed Potato Tots or the Chicken-Fried Buffalo Steak. Best secret: Shiner Bock Beer Bread and Ms. Helen Corbitt's Pimento Cheese Popover.

The Ranch at Las Colinas: 857 W. John Carpenter Freeway, Irving
972-506-7262 ● www.theranchic.com
Stampede 66: 1717 McKinney Avenue, Dallas ● 214-550-6966
www.stampede66.com
Twin Peaks: 5260 Belt Line Road, Addison ● 972-503-7325
www.twinpeaksrestaurant.com

WAGE WAR
AGAINST CANCER AT THE CATTLE BARON'S BALL

The Cattle Baron's Ball is always a stellar evening. Everyone should experience this "event of the year" at least once! Southfork Ranch has hosted the fabulous Western-themed event for years.

Committee members work tirelessly year-round to find the choicest auction items (while they are searching for that perfect Western-flavored outfit). The biggest draw is the mega-wattage country music star who takes the stage after the bidding, eating, and gambling. The Cattle Baron's Ball is called the world's largest single-night benefit for cancer research. With the 2013 total of $1.3 million raised (and $50 million since 1974), you can see why. A sprinkle or even buckets of rain will not slow down this party. If it storms, the entertainers crank up the music and increase the beer flow. Muddy boots don't matter. This is the ultimate gala, rain or shine. The Ball's success reflects the generosity of the revelers. Tickets aren't cheap, but it's a good cause.

214-443-9222 • www.cattlebaronsball.com

Tip:

Catch a trolley bus for the one-hour narrated JFK Assassination Tour, Wednesday through Sunday. Sights include the motorcade route, Oswald time-line route, J. D. Tippit murder scene, Oswald's boarding house, Texas Theater, Old Dallas City Jail, and Jack Ruby's Carousel Club. You've read about it, now see it firsthand. The JFK Memorial, designed by Philip Johnson, is a few blocks away behind the Old Red Courthouse . . . a good place to reflect on the great loss to the world and Dallas.

LEARN ABOUT "THAT FATEFUL DAY"
AT THE SIXTH FLOOR MUSEUM

In 1963, the Texas School Book Depository was just a non-descript building near a grassy knoll. In that year, on November 22, we lost a president, and the nation stood still, especially Dallas. The Sixth Floor Museum, located in the former Depository building, is a stunning piece of unforgettable history. All the documentation is chronicled here: the assassination and legacy of President John F. Kennedy; artifacts, photos, films, evidence, and eyewitness accounts adding up to about 40,000 items. There is the eeriness of actually seeing the sniper's nest. Open daily except Thanksgiving and Christmas.

Dealey Plaza: 411 Elm St., Dallas • 214-747-6660 • www.jfk.org

HAVE COCKTAILS
ON THE PATIO AT SAINT ANN COURT

Saint Ann Court, built as a Catholic school in 1927, is easy on the eyes with its terraced grounds and sculptured shrub gardens. The live music adds a special vibe. This is romantic al fresco dining at its best, with easy access from Wolf to Harwood Street.

Saint Ann: 2501 North Harwood, Dallas ● 214-782-9807
www.saintanndallas.com

Visit the Samurai Collection next door to Saint Ann. This collection has several hundred excellent examples of old Samurai armor and weaponry, from as early as the tenth century. The delicately crafted armor is dynamic and beautiful. Be sure to have your parking ticket validated. Closed on Mondays.

GET ARTSY
AT THE BISHOP ARTS DISTRICT

The Bishop Arts District is adorned with quaint, interesting, and locally owned and operated cafes, coffee houses, shops, galleries, small bars, and niche clothing stores. You'll want to spend time in the Artisan's Collective, and a few yummy minutes in Dude, Sweet Chocolate. This is not your grandmother's Oak Cliff. On Bastille Day, July 14, revel in a fantastic street festival to entertain all the Francophiles. Lucia Restaurant is so popular you need a reservation weeks in advance. The Texas Theater is a shining piece of Art Deco history that shows off-beat films. Stop by the nearby Art Deco Belmont Hotel Patio for the best view of the skyline after dark.

1230 W. Davis St., Dallas • 214-272-8346 • www.bishopartsdistrict.com

The Kessler Theater, in the Bishop Arts District, continues to get rave reviews for being the "best listening room" for hearing top-notch bands. With a cool bar and a kitchen that serves up tasty selections, you are all set. There are also restaurants within walking distance. There's always a nice-looking crowd getting a live music fix at the Kessler.

PICK YOUR TEAM
IN THE BATTLE FOR THE IRON SKILLET

The Horned Frogs and Mustangs have played some classics over the years. The rivalry game between the two former Southwest Conference teams alternates annually between Gerald Ford Stadium on the SMU campus and Amon Carter Stadium on the TCU campus. The teams have met most years (all but six) since the rivalry first started in 1915, with TCU holding a slight edge. In 1946, the Iron Skillet was proposed as "a symbol of the rivalry and a substitute for vandalism" carried out by fans on both campuses the previous year. Tailgating (called Boulevarding at SMU) is a play-all-day event with cheerleaders, food booths, games, and music. TCU Tailgating has its own special purple and white, pre and post, parking lot parties.

Gerald Ford Stadium: 5800 Ownby Dr., Dallas • 214-768-1617
www.smumustangs.com

Amon Carter Stadium: 2850 Stadium Dr., Fort Worth • 817-257-3764
www.gofrogs.com

RIDE RIDES
AT THE STATE FAIR, OR VISIT FAIR PARK YEAR-ROUND

Step right up and get your "deep-fried everything," from fried ice cream or fried guacamole to everyone's favorite, Fletcher's Corny Dogs. State Fair of Texas fans have to say howdy to the new Big Tex, due to the original going up in flames in 2012. Fair Park claims to have one of the world's tallest tower rides and one of North America's tallest Ferris wheels, the Texas Star. Plan on spending some m-o-n-e-y.

Fair Park has wonderful Art Deco façades, performance facilities, and a lagoon. "Cool Zones" and a surf rider have been added for Summertime Adventures. The museums include the majestic Hall of State, African American Museum, Perot Museum at Fair Park, Children's Aquarium, Texas Discovery Gardens, and the South Dallas Cultural Center. The Firefighter's Museum is outside the gates. Fair Park is open seven days a week year-round.

1121 First Ave., Dallas ● 214-426-3400 ● www.fairpark.org

SHOP
'TIL YOU HAVE TO STOP

Those who live "lifestyles of the rich and famous" come from all over the world simply to shop upscale boutiques. Shopping is one of Dallas's favorite pastimes. You'll discover diamonds, furnishings, fashions, and unique treasures here found nowhere else in the world. Locally-owned by Crawford Brock and his family, Stanley Korshak is an independent department store loved for Dallas luxury shopping. Located in Dallas's grand Crescent Hotel, Stanley Korshak has three additional shops located in the courtyard: Bridal Salon (world-famous designer gowns), The Home Shop, and The Shak for contemporary fashions. The Copper Lamp at Preston/Royal has everything fabulous except copper. The array of sterling silver, crystal, and estate pieces will surprise first-time shoppers. It's possibly the best place in Dallas to find wedding gifts. The Write Selection is the perfect boutique to discover the gift for your rich friend who has everything or St. Michael's Woman's Exchange, a popular "retail ministry" for over 50 years. You may just bump into a celebrity like Laura Bush, Jessica Simpson, or Oprah at Forty Five Ten, the mecca of boutiques with an international reputation for offering the best of the best.

The Copper Lamp
6025 Royal Lane #208, Dallas, 214-369-5166
www.copperlamp.com

Forty Five Ten
4510 McKinney Ave., Dallas, 214-559-4510
www.fortyfiveten.com

St. Michael's Woman's Exchange
5 Highland Park Village, Dallas, 214-521-3862
www.st.-michaels-womans-exchange.com

Stanley Korshak
500 Crescent Court, Suite 100, Dallas, 214-871-3600
www.stanleykorshak.com

Write Selection
314 Preston Royal Village, Dallas, 214-750-0531
www.writeselection.net

For more retail therapy, we are crazy about
the treasures found at these wonderful shops: It's the
Arrangement and Anteks for fantastic Southwestern furnishings
and accessories. Southwest Gallery has a dazzling array of all types of
fine art for sale. Pinto Ranch at NorthPark Center will outfit everyone
in boots, belts, hats, and everything Western. For women's couture,
check out Tootsie's at Preston Center. Elements on Lover's Lane and
Allie Coosh in Snider Plaza are favorites of Park Cities' shoppers.
West Village, Inwood Village, and Southlake Town Square have a
variety of upscale shops. The Shops at Legacy will help complete
your shopping list. Afterward, you can sip a libation at
the Blue Martini Lounge.

GET KNIGHTED
AT THE SCARBOROUGH RENAISSANCE FAIRE

This ultimate medieval festival features twenty-one stages of performers and endless audience participation. Fairgoers are encouraged to dress in period costumes, and don't be surprised by the varied choices—tavern maids, pirates, Game of Thrones, and you name it. Hard-core fans spend thousands of bucks to be authentic. They never get out of character nor lose their faux dialects. Besides the fun and bizarre costumes, there are craftsmen at work, unique shopping opportunities, and terrific food booths. Tickets are pricey, plus you will want extra spending cash. The parking area is dry and dusty, or a bit muddy if it rains. But all in all this is an unforgettable experience for kids and adults.

2511 FM 66, Waxahachie • 972-938-3247 • www.srfestival.com

RECONNECT WITH NATURE
AT THE TRINITY FOREST ADVENTURE PARK

Escape the concrete jungle in seven acres of fun in the Great Trinity Forest. This adventure park is unique for Texas and consists of ziplines, cargo nets, bridges, climbing features, and balance beams. There are sixty platforms, six courses, and four levels of difficulty suited to challenge every type of ability and fitness. Climb, zip, soar, and drop in a canopy of two hundred-year-old post oak trees. Great for birthdays or team building. Reservations are strongly recommended.

1820 Dowdy Ferry Rd. • 214-398-3400 • www.trinitytreetops.com

VISIT THE FABULOSO
LATINO CULTURAL CENTER ... OLE'

The stunning architecture of the building alone is worth seeing. The architect's use of brilliant color and light are an integral part of the design, with its tower, plaza, fountain, and portico. This Arts and Culture Center represents the best of Latino artists in film, theater, visual arts, and literature. Designed by Ricardo Legorreta, the center is a regional catalyst for preserving Latino and Hispanic arts and culture. There are about 300 events at the center each year, many held in its large theater. It is operated by the City of Dallas Office of Cultural Affairs.

2600 Live Oak St., Dallas ● 214-671-0045 ● www.latinoculturalcenter.org

FEEL THE VITALITY
OF SHOPPING AT NORTHPARK CENTER

With 235 retailers, NorthPark Center is one of the retail wonders of the modern world. Designer shopping, restaurants, fun people-watching, incredible sculptures, a garden, and a first-class movie house are available. This is like a huge indoor Rodeo Drive. NorthPark Center features a magnificent backdrop of art, architecture, and landscaping. In 2006 there was a $250 million expansion, raising its size to 1.2 million square feet. Hard to believe, but it is being super-sized again. Dallasites love, love, love NorthPark Center. Valet parking, luxury car washes, and tax-free shopping for international visitors are available.

8687 N. Central Expressway, Dallas • 214-363-7441

www.northparkcenter.com

PREPARE TO SAY "WOW"
ON AN AT&T STADIUM TOUR

A must-do. You have to see the ultimate sports palace, known as a "Mecca" to true Dallas Cowboys fans. You don't have to be a Cowboys/Jerry Jones fan to be awed by this stadium. Its sheer size is stunning. Well, you know the saying: "Go Big or Go Home." The huge HD Jumbotron is a jaw-dropping sight. Super Bowl XLV, the NBA All-Star Game, the Final Four, the College Football Playoff Title Game, the Cotton Bowl, and numerous sold-out concerts are among the events that have been or will be held here. The billion-dollar behemoth began as a dream to change the way fans watch games. One of the most exciting innovations is the collection of large-scale museum-quality art displayed throughout the structure—forty-six works by thirty-five artists. Self-guided and VIP tours available.

1 Legends Way, Arlington • 817-892-4000
www.stadium.dallascowboys.com

Dee Lincoln's Tasting Room & Bubble Bar is on the Silver Suite Level. It's the first of its kind in a sports arena anywhere in the world. Forty-eight wines are dispensed at the perfect temperature, allowing patrons to experience wines by the ounce. Bubbles by the glass and creative martinis are also fun!

MARVEL AT THE MUSIC
AT THE MEYERSON SYMPHONY CENTER

Home to the wonderful Dallas Symphony Orchestra, this I.M. Pei–designed building has stunning architectural features and excellent acoustics. This landmark in the Arts District receives accolades from the international press and rivals the great concert halls of the world. Every note sounds good, regardless of your seat. The centerpiece is the McDermott Concert Hall, which has a "shoebox" design, contributing to the intimacy between performers and the audience. The focal point is the Lay Family Concert Organ with almost 5,000 pipes.

2301 Flora St., Dallas • 214-692-0203 • www.dallassymphony.com

BASK IN THE GLOW
OF THE STRATOSPHERICALLY WEALTHY IN HIGHLAND PARK AND UNIVERSITY PARK

From the shiny new McMansions to the lovingly preserved old grand-dame homes, it's all good in the Park Cities. Nicknamed "The Bubble," Park Cities is divided by Preston Road, which was the first paved street and one of the first major highways in this area. The Holidays draw thousands of people who oooh and aaah over the incredible light displays. Hop a romantic carriage ride during December. In spring time the neighborhood is ablaze with azaleas. Highland Park Village, one of the oldest shopping centers in the United States, dates back to the early 1930s and was placed on the National Historic Landmarks List in 2000. When someone says, "Highland Park Village," we think couture, couture, couture. Have a Starbucks latte outside and watch the stream of beautiful luxury cars and beautiful people.

Preston Rd. and Mockingbird Lane, Dallas • 214-272-4874

www.hpvillage.com

LOVE SOME LONGHORNS
AT THE STOCKYARDS NATIONAL HISTORIC DISTRICT

Our suggestion is to spend the night at the Stockyards Hotel (historic, with themed rooms) in the heart of one of Texas's most beloved historic areas. That will allow you to soak up all the folklore and history in Stockyards Station. There are walking tours, Longhorn cattle drives twice a day, a cattle pen maze, Texas Cowboy Hall of Fame, the Livestock Exchange Building, restaurants, bars, a concert venue, horseback riding, and best of all, Billy Bob's Texas dance hall. It's a slice of Texas heritage, and there's nothing quite like it anywhere.

E. Exchange Ave., Fort Worth, 817-624-4741, www.fortworthstockyards.org

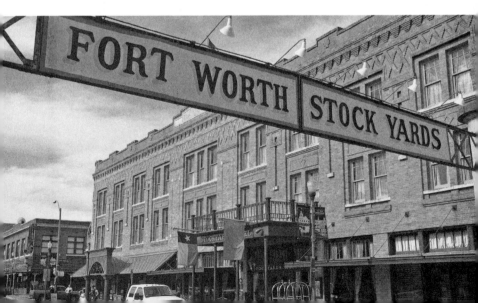

CATCH THE PGA TOUR
AT THE HP BYRON NELSON CHAMPIONSHIP AND COLONIAL INVITATIONAL

Four Seasons Resort and Club is one of Texas's most luxurious spots in Las Colinas. The normal tour date is usually sometime in May. Lord Byron is no longer with us, but his memory lives on in this exciting 72-hole event, Thursday to Sunday. Bring your walking shoes and plenty of sunscreen because there are large spaces without trees. A special treat is the "Pavilion After Dark Concert Series," which extends the fun after the tournament concludes. The following Thursday-Sunday, if you aren't golfed out, head to the Crowne Plaza Invitational at the Colonial in Fort Worth, where Ben Hogan once ruled. This is a tighter, more mature course near TCU. Expect a more conservative, but perhaps savvier golf crowd than at the Byron Nelson, which is a Dallas to-be-seen swanky spot.

The fifth hole at the Colonial, which runs alongside the Trinity River, is considered one of the toughest in America.

TPC Four Seasons: 4150 N. MacArthur Blvd., Irving ● 972-717-0700
www.hpbnc.org

Colonial Country Club: 3735 Country Club Circle, Fort Worth ● 817-927-4201, www.colonialfw.com

EAT YOUR WAY
ACROSS ADDISON

In addition to 118 acres of parks and over 4,000 hotel rooms, Addison boasts more than 170 restaurants. Celebrity Chef Richard Chamberlain turns out culinary delights at both Chamberlain's Fish Market Grill (voted Diner's Choice Winner) and Chamberlain's Steak & Chop House (voted Best of DFW Steakhouses). A Dallas legend, Arthur's is one of the most beautiful fine dining restaurants, with chandeliers, dark rich woods, and even an aquarium as one wall. The bar is a great place for dancing and meeting people. Gloria's Restaurant blends Latin, Salvadorian, Mexican, and Tex-Mex cuisines all in one fun place. The patio is always packed so show up early. The Salsa nights are a best-kept secret. A fun fact: Every resident in the town of Addison could go to the 170 restaurants at once and all could be seated.

Chamberlain's Fish Market Grill
4525 Belt Line Rd., Addison, 972-503-3474
www.chamberlainsseafood.com

Chamberlain's Steak and Chop House
5330 Belt Line Rd., Addison, 972-934-2467
www.chamberlainssteakhouse.com

Arthur's Prime Steaks and Seafood
15175 Quorum Dr., Addison, 972-385-0800
www.arthursdallas.com

Gloria's Latin Cuisine
5100 Belt Line Rd., Addison, 972-387-8442
www.gloriasrestaurants.com

Jaxx Steakhouse is an excellent place for a dinner of steaks, seafood, and pasta in a 1930s Boston atmosphere. The narrow bar is the place to be. Join the regulars in the cozy confines that remind you of a different era when the "saloon keep" tended bar and kept the bourbon flowing. At the back of the bar are numerous memorabilia and pictures of Mickey Mantle, the late New York Yankee's baseball star, who lived in Dallas during his later years. Jaxx was one of his favorite spots. Here's to you, Mick.

14925 Midway Rd., #101, Addison, 972-458-7888
www.jaxxsteakhouse.com

"KISS ME, I'M IRISH"
AT THE ST. PATRICK'S DAY PARADE

If you can't get to NOLA for Mardi Gras, then maybe you can wear your ugliest green to one of the largest St. Pat's parades in the Southwest. There's something for everyone's taste on Greenville Avenue, with over one hundred floats, many quite outrageous. It falls on the Saturday preceding St. Patrick's Day. There are more than 100,000 revelers having a play day on Greenville Avenue, plus a party after the parade with bars open 'til 2 a.m. Oh sure . . . like you haven't already had enough green beer!

Greenville Avenue, Dallas • www.greenvilleave.org

SAVE MONEY
BY SPENDING IT AT SAM MOON

If you are a neophyte to Sam Moon, then you are about to become a convert. This warehouse-like store at Harry Hines and LBJ Freeway is brimming full of accessories. We mean tons of jewelry, handbags, luggage, faux hair, and things you didn't know you wanted. The walls-upon-walls of items are well organized, and the prices so affordable that you can buy multiples without buyer's remorse. This is a girly-girl place, so in order not to be rushed, just leave your male companion behind. The shop next door is named the Luggage Shop, but that is a misnomer because it is full of crafts, games, novelties, college and kid's items. The Texas-based chain, known for deep discounts, has expanded to many other sister stores in several states.

11826 Harry Hines Blvd., Dallas • 972-484-3084 • www.sammoon.com

BET THE TRIFECTA
AT LONE STAR PARK

Experience North Texas's version of thoroughbred horse racing. The amenities are excellent in the club level, Silks, with your choice of buffets or menus. There are some big-name jockeys who race here, so come and enjoy the excitement from early April through early July. There are usually several post-race concerts with well-known bands, vocalists, and fireworks during the three-month racing season. Lone Star Park's Bar & Book is open seven days a week, year-round, offering simulcast racing action from around the country. There's a fall quarter horse racing schedule as well.

1000 Lone Star Parkway, Grand Prairie • 972-263-RACE
www.lonestarpark.com

HEY KIDS, TAKE YOUR PARENTS
TO THE ARBORETUM'S CHILDREN'S ADVENTURE GARDEN

Here it is, finally . . . a rival to the Perot Museum of Nature and Science and possibly the coolest family attraction in the whole state. The $62 million, eight-acre Rory Meyers Children's Adventure Garden includes seventeen galleries (learning rooms) and 150 hands-on exhibits and trails that wind through a woodland ecosystem. The Exploration Center encompasses 9,100 square feet. The Garden for Kids is an enormous expansion to the Arboretum, which overlooks White Rock Lake on sixty-six acres, and comprises one of the most beautiful gardens in the world. Each season has its own unique color changes and beauty. Springtime has 500,000 blooming bulbs. This is the ultimate escape and the perfect place to become rejuvenated!

It doesn't get better than spring, summer, and fall concerts at the Arboretum. The views of White Rock Lake are awesome. Bring your family, friends, and favorite picnic selections.

8525 Garland Rd., Dallas • 214-515-6500
www.dallasarboretum.org

Campisi's Egyptian Restaurant

(multiple locations)
The original: 5610
E. Mockingbird
Lane, Dallas, 214-827-0355
www.campisis.com

Javier's Gourmet Mexicano

4912 Cole Ave., Dallas, 214-521-4211
www.javiers.net

Keller's Drive-In Hamburgers

(multiple locations)
6537 E. Northwest Highway, Dallas, 214-368-1209

Terilli's

2815 Greenville Ave., Dallas, 214-827-3993
www.terillis.com

RELISH
DALLAS'S LEGENDARY RESTAURANTS

Dallas landmark Terilli's offers a fantastic patio with a downtown view. Jeannie Terilli's secret recipe makes her signature, fresh-daily Italchos, a combination of nachos and pizza, an amazing culinary indulgence for decades. The original Campisi's Egyptian Restaurant was started in 1946 when Carlo "Papa" Campisi created a "pizza pie" rumored to be Dallas's and Texas's first pizza. His son, Joe, carried on the legend and made sure Campisi's was granted one of the first liquor licenses in the State of Texas since Prohibition. Today, David Campisi has expanded the award-winning concept to multiple locations. *Bon Appetit* named Campisi's one of the best pizzerias in America. Javier's Gourmet Mexicano, tucked away in Highland Park, is famous for traditional Mexican food. Voted Top 10 burger in America by CNN, Keller's Hamburgers is a six-decade legend for its flavorful patties on poppy seed buns.

DISCOVER
FORT WORTH'S FAMOUS PLACES FOR STEAKS

Fort Worth is known as an important stop for cattle drives along the Chisholm Trail, so no surprise beef is king. In Cowtown, Tim Love is nationally renowned for his steaks (our favorite is the Roasted Garlic Stuffed Beef Tenderloin) served in a casual setting at Lonesome Dove, which has been voted the best lunch value in Fort Worth. Since 1947, Cattlemen's Steak House in Fort Worth's Historic Stockyards is known for its aged, corn-fed cattle charcoal-grilled steaks. If you want a great steak in a more contemporary setting, go to Grace Restaurant for the Meyer Ranch Filet. The cow is naturally raised on grass and finished on corn with an all-vegetarian diet with no motorized vehicles on the ranch. Besides the "melt in your mouth" steaks at Bob's Steak & Chop House, you will love the Texas-sized carrot that comes on the side. At Del Frisco's Double Eagle Steak House, try an Australian Cold Water Lobster Tail.

Bob's Steak & Chop House
1300 Houston St., Fort Worth, 817-350-4100
www.bobs-steakandchop.com
Other area locations: Dallas, Grapevine and Plano

Cattlemen's Steak House
2458 North Main St., Fort Worth, 817-624-3945
www.cattlemenssteakhouse.com

Del Frisco's Double Eagle Steak House
812 Main St., Fort Worth, 817-877-3999
www.delfriscos.com
Another location in Far North Dallas

Grace
777 Main St., Fort Worth, 817-877-3388
www.gracefortworth.com

Lonesome Dove Western Bistro
2406 N. Main St., Fort Worth, 817-740-8810
www.lonesomedovebistro.com

STUDY BLACK HISTORY AND CULTURE
AT THE AFRICAN AMERICAN MUSEUM

This is an example of Dallas's many one-of-a-kind institutions. There is not even another museum like this in the entire Southwest region. Founded in 1974 at the cost of $7 million and financed mainly through donations, the 36,000-square-foot structure houses a permanent collection of folk art and historical archives, with four galleries, a theater, and classrooms. The museum's building is made of ivory stone and is configured in the shape of a cross.

3536 Grand Ave., Fair Park, Dallas • 214-565-9026 • www.aamdallas.org

JOIN
ONE OF THE NOVEL TOURS
TO SEE DALLAS

Thousands of locals and visitors have learned about this municipality on a fully narrated downtown trolley tour, which is really a bus, painted like a trolley. Highlights on the one-hour, fifteen-minute tour are: West End, Klyde Warren Park, Pioneer Plaza, Thanksgiving Square, Flagship Neiman Marcus, John Neely Bryan's Log Cabin, Arts District, Reunion Tower, Meyerson Symphony Hall, Margaret Hunt Hill Bridge, and Perot Museum. Ask your tour guide about the four Pritzker prize–winning architectural buildings, all on one block.

Choices are Trolley Bus, Segway, Cultural Walking, Chocolate, Uptown Food Tours, Skyline Tours, and the JFK Assassination Tour.

www.bigdfuntours.com • www.toursdallas.net
www.dallasbychocolate.com • www.fundallastours.com
www.dallassegwaytours.com

SOAK UP SOME CULTURE
AT THE DALLAS ARTS DISTRICT

Dallasites have always had legitimate bragging rights, but especially today, due to the $15 billion development of "the country's largest urban arts district." There is a plethora of things to do in this nineteen-block area, thanks to thirty years in the making, and deep pockets of many wealthy donors. There are seventeen venues, three of those are museums: Perot Museum of Nature and Science, Dallas Museum of Art, and the Nasher Sculpture Center. The famed Meyerson Symphony Hall, Winspear Opera House, Dee and Charles Wyly Theatre, Trammell Crow Collection, and others are in the mix as well. You will only scratch the surface by spending half a day here. Whether it's art, theater, music, sculptures, parks, museums, or dining, everything is walkable, clean, and safe. Check out the events calendar.

Arts District Office: 2200 Ross Ave., Dallas • 214-744-6642
www.downtowndallas.org

RACE FANS,
START YOUR ENGINES
AT TEXAS MOTOR SPEEDWAY

It's worth it to spend a weekend in northern Fort Worth when the NASCAR Sprint Car Series hits town in the spring and fall of each year at the track. Thousands of people flock to the oval in various campers and motor homes. They party hardy before, during, and after the races. Whether you love or hate NASCAR the fact remains that these cars are moving at incredible speeds. The Speedway Club has creative dining/cocktail specialties. Try the Smokin' Hubcaps or the Bacon Cotton Candy Martini. For those who want to feel the sensation of driving a real race car, check out www.totaldrivingexperience.com. There are also informative tours available.

"Big Hoss," the world's largest HD screen, is an exciting addition coming to the Speedway. If you like statistics, here goes: It's 9,000 square feet larger than Jumbotron at AT&T Cowboy Stadium, bigger than the Lincoln Memorial, and weighs more than seven elephants. Construction will be complete in April 2014. Just leave the binoculars at home.

3545 Lone Star Circle, Fort Worth ● 817-215-8500
www.texasmotorspeedway.com

SIP AND GRAZE
AT SAVOR DALLAS AND THE BEAUJOLAIS FESTIVAL

Big Fun, Big Flavor . . . Savor Dallas is called "the most delicious food and wine festival in Texas." Locals and guests have come from across the country to celebrate wine, food, spirits, and the arts in downtown Dallas and nearby for a decade and counting. The festival was founded by culinary and wine lovers Jim and Vicki Briley-White. With more than sixty-five top chefs and hundreds of premium wines, spirits, and beers, this event stays exciting with new settings each year. Multiple venues from the Arts District to the Arboretum help keep it fun but upscale. The largest event, the International Grand Tasting, attracts more than 2,500 foodies and wine lovers. There are several days in March of activities including seminars. Vino lovers look forward to tasting the new Beaujolais each November at an event sponsored by the French-American Chamber of Commerce. Be there for all the cork popping.

888-728-6747 • www.savordallas.com
972-241-0111 • www.faccdallas.com

JOG ON AN ABANDONED RAILROAD TRACK
AT THE KATY TRAIL

You will see all sorts of activities besides jogging in this 3.5-mile linear park: walking, running, in-line skating, biking, and, of course, dog walking. There are more than a dozen public entrances and plazas linking Katy Trail to other area parks. There are 125 contiguous acres in this popular parkland, which is located in the heart of Dallas. Take a break from your exercise on the twelve-foot-wide trail and refuel at the Katy Trail Ice House. It's a casual, Austin-type experience, serving brews, barbeque, venison chili, and other specialties. Well-behaved dogs are welcome in this outdoor venue. It's great for watching girls in short shorts and men with six-pack abs.

214-303-1180 • www.katytraildallas.org

SEE THE $30 MILLION GIANTS OF THE SAVANNA
AT THE DALLAS ZOO

The crown jewel at the Dallas Zoo is the awesome Savanna exhibit, a natural habitat to see the big African beauties up close and personal. Watching a small herd of giraffes running or feeding them out of your hand is breathtaking. The keepers give periodic talks. Morning is a great time to go with shorter lines and more active animals. It's fun to watch your favorite critters at feeding time. Don't miss the Koala Walkabout, the only one in Texas. Get a bird's eye view when you ride the monorail. The DART Red Line drops you off at the door.

650 South R.L. Thornton Freeway, Dallas • 469-554-7500
www.dallaszoo.com

BE AWED
BY THE PEROT MUSEUM OF NATURE AND SCIENCE

Dinosaurs! Space! Nature! No matter your age, prepare to be inspired by this 180,000-square-foot "World of Wonder," five-story showplace near the Arts District. The generosity of the Ross Perot family made this dream a reality. A two-hour visit becomes a live lesson regarding all things nature and science. There are lots of exciting hands-on exhibits. You can virtually race T-Rex or learn about extreme weather in 3-D. The bottom floor is dedicated to very young patrons: it is smaller and engaging. There are six learning labs, an auditorium, outdoor play space, and a courtyard. The museum is "clean and green" and has a food court and the obligatory gift shop. You'll likely either love or hate the ultra contemporary architecture, but who doesn't love controversy?

2201 N. Field St., Dallas • 214-428-5555 • www.perotmuseum.org

FIND OUT
WHY NOTHING EQUALS
A DALLAS COWBOYS GAME

While AT&T Stadium auditions for a spot among the Eight Wonders of the World, the Dallas Cowboys will try to play their way into the Super Bowl and win another World Championship. Annually, the Cowboys play eight regular-season games and at least two exhibition games in Arlington. There's really not a bad seat in the stadium, and the amenities even on the highest level outclass all competing venues. Cowboys provide customized maps for navigating the traffic and getting to the parking lots of your choice, either cash lots or pre-purchased parking pass for specific lots. Go to www.dallascowboysmaps. com for instructions.

AT&T Stadium: 1 Legends Way, Arlington • www.dallascowboys.com

Tip:

The AT&T Cotton Bowl Classic
is played in AT&T Stadium in late
December or early January each year
with two of the top teams in college
football competing. The semifinals and
national championship games of the
College Football Playoff are held here
intermittently.

SCOOT YOUR BOOTS
AT SOME GREAT DANCE HALLS

Billy Bob's Texas in Fort Worth is a rite of passage out West. It could be called an indoor resort. It's crazy big. This dance hall has bull riding, pool tables, gaming, house bands, shopping, line dancing, and BBQ. The concerts start late: 10:30 p.m. Cover charges change according to which artist is appearing. They have a great memorabilia wall from past performers. Expect lots of hats, boots, and general rowdiness.

Gilley's (South Side Music Hall) is Dallas's answer to Billy Bob's Texas, but Fort Worth wins the size contest. Sons of Hermann Hall is another authentic honky-tonk for swing dancing and lessons. The 100-year-old spot is called the "best place to take a non-Texan." It is as comfortable as an old shoe and rumored to be haunted. Open Wednesdays through Sundays.

Billy Bob's: 2520 Rodeo Plaza, Fort Worth • 817-624-7117
www.billybobstexas.com
Gilley's: 1136 S. Lamar St., Dallas • 214-421-2021
www.gilleysdallas.com
Sons of Hermann Hall: 3414 Elm St., Dallas • 214-747-4422
www.sonsofhermann.com

TAKE YOUR MAMA FOR SOME DRAMA
AT THE WINSPEAR OPERA HOUSE OR THE WYLY THEATRE

The Winspear Opera House (AT&T Performing Arts Center) is a perfect reinvention of the traditional opera house. It is completely stunning. From the brilliant red exterior to the inspirational retracting chandelier, this is a fitting venue for a city filled with performing arts fans. Comfortable seats, excellent sound system, and several bars. In addition to world-class operas, the Winspear Opera House brings Broadway shows, the Texas Ballet Company, concerts, and comedians to the stage.

The Dee and Charles Wyly Theatre (Dallas Theatre Center) receives raves for its award-winning architecture; think sleek contemporary. There are 600 seats in a multiform setting. The floor can reconfigure in the middle of a production with a small crew. It is one of the most versatile theatrical performing spaces in the world. The local performing company is a powerhouse. Enjoy first-rate productions, bar service, and easy accessibility to the parking garage. There are free tours of both venues on first Saturdays.

2403 Flora St., Dallas ● 214-880-0202 ● www.attpac.org
2400 Flora St., Dallas ● 214-526-8210 ● www.dallastheatercenter.org

Nick & Sam's Steakhouse
3008 Maple Ave., Dallas, 214-871-7444
www.nick-sams.com

Al Biernat's
4217 Oak Lawn Ave., Dallas, 214-219-2201
www.albiernats.com

III Forks
17776 Dallas Pkwy., Dallas, 972-267-1776
www.IIIforks.com

CHANNEL YOUR INNER CARNIVORE
WITH DALLAS'S BEST STEAKS

As Julia Child said, "The only time to eat diet food is while you're waiting for the steak to cook." Cattle ranching has been a major Texas industry for three centuries. Guests come from all over the world to indulge in a juicy steak. The bigger, the better. At Nick & Sam's Steakhouse, the favorite is Samir Dhurandhar's dry-aged "Long Bone" Cowboy with black truffle butter. The steaks come from Allen Brothers, the Chicago-based, century-old, steak Mecca known for hand-cut, hand-selected U.S. Prime beef. Check out Nick & Sam's co-owner Joe Palladino's extensive wine collection autographed by famous actors and sports celebrities. Try the Lobster Mac & Cheese. Caviar is free. Al Biernat's Restaurant is known for prime rib. A local "see and be seen" place, Biernat's is a favorite for celebrities. For a Las Vegas atmosphere, head to III Forks Steakhouse where you will enjoy over 25,000 square feet of Texas French cuisine.

ADMIRE THE ARTS
IN THE FORT WORTH CULTURAL DISTRICT

Two million visitors a year from all over the world can't be wrong. Just minutes from downtown Fort Worth, you'll find tree-lined boulevards leading to an area alive with entertainment, art, science, and exhibit buildings that house countless treasures. Six world-class museums all in one setting: Science and History Museum, Amon Carter Museum, Cattle Raisers Museum, Modern Art Museum, Kimbell Art Museum, National Cowgirl Museum, and even a Department Store Museum. You will work up an appetite, and there are twelve restaurants surrounding the arts district. There are venues for Broadway shows, plays, operas, concerts, rodeos, horse shows, and an occasional circus: Casa Manana, Equestrian Center, Omni Theater, Will Rogers Center, and others.

Camp Bowie area, Fort Worth • 817-336-5812 • www.fwculture.com

GET SPIRITUAL
AT THE BIBLICAL ARTS CENTER

A treasure trove of art with a Biblical theme awaits you here, including one of the rarest Bible collections in the world. The art is varied, and it's a cultural crossroads with sculptures, drawings, fine prints, and oils. Artists include Marc Chagall, John Singer Sargent, and Andy Warhol. A fire destroyed the museum in 2006, and 2,500 works were lost. Today the Biblical Arts Center is bigger and better than ever with 30,000 square feet. There is nothing quite like it in the United States. It is across the street from NorthPark Center, and tickets are $12 for regular admission and $10 for students and seniors.

7500 Park Lane, Dallas ● 214-368-4622 ● www.biblicalarts.org

How about attending the Gospel Brunch
at the House of Blues after touring the Biblical Arts Center?
Local talent performs traditional and contemporary songs.
There is an all-you-can-eat brunch. Hallelujah.

SPEND A DAY
AT THE DALLAS FARMER'S MARKET

Farmers have been selling produce on the site of the Dallas Farmer's Market since the late 1800s. As Dallas grew, the demand for farm-fresh produce increased. In 1939, the site was formalized, and the first shed was established. Today, the Dallas Farmer's Market features all-fresh, locally-grown produce from Texas farmers. The way it should be! At this major Dallas attraction you can spend all day chatting with farmers, shopping, and eating all things Texan. This Dallas landmark is being completely transformed. Considered "the next big redevelopment opportunity for downtown Dallas," the market is becoming one of the area's most exciting entertainment districts and neighborhoods featuring innovative residences, restaurants with name chefs, retail shops, an athletic field, and community gardens.

1010 S. Pearl Expressway, Dallas ● 214-670-5879
www.dallasfarmersmarket.org

HOP A RIDE FROM UPTOWN OR DOWNTOWN
ON THE FREE M-LINE TROLLEY

These restored heritage streetcars, dating back to 1909, are one of Dallas's best assets. The four different air-conditioned cars, connecting Uptown to Downtown since 1989, even have names: Rosie, Green Dragon, Matilda, and Petunia. Others being restored are the Winnie and the Morning Star. A new car, Betty, has recently been added. They deliver passengers to twenty-eight points of interest and have twenty-eight different boarding and de-boarding stops. The M-Line was founded by restaurateur Phil Cobb. After a planned extension is done, MATA (McKinney Avenue Transit Authority) will stop inside the Klyde Warren Park and travel close to DART's Pearl Street Station. The trolleys are available for charter for a fee. The M-Line runs seven days a week, and on holidays. It's free and it's fun. Did we remember to tell you it's free?

Headquarters: 3153 Oak Grove Ave., Dallas • 214-855-0006
www.mata.org

CHANNEL YOUR INNER JAMES BOND
IN AN EXOTIC CAR

"Keep up with the Jones's" while you enjoy your Dallas experience. On every corner in Uptown, Highland Park, and Plano, you'll be overwhelmed with the glitz of stretch limos and fast cars of every color and style. You too need to demand this kind of attention. Channel your inner James Bond at Benny Black's Platinum Motorcars. It's not your everyday car dealership! Here, you can rent luxury and exotic vehicles such as a Rolls Royce Phantom, Rolls Royce Ghost, Lamborghini Performante, Gallardo Spyder, 458 Italia, Ferrari 430 Spyder, Bentley GTC & Continental, and a Porsche Turbo, among others. Another place to purchase these racy jewels is Scott Ginsburg's Boardwalk Auto Group. He sells imports from Lamborghinis to Maserati's, Ferrari's and Fiats. "Experts in Excellence," Park Place Motorcars is a Dallas favorite for the ever-popular Lexus. For the cutting-edge, newly-released Aston Martin, visit Aston Martin of Dallas.

Aston Martin of Dallas
5333 Lemmon Ave., Dallas, 214-522-1007
www.astonmartin.com

Boardwalk Auto Group
6300 International Parkway, Plano, 972-447-5200
www.boardwalkautogroup.com

Park Place Motorcars
6113 Lemmon Ave., Dallas, 214-526-8701
www.parkplacetexas.com

Platinum Motorcars
11430 N. Central Expressway, Dallas, 469-374-9090
www.platinummotorcars.com

All Aboard!

This elaborate holiday model train exhibit at NorthPark has 4,000 square feet of track with themed realistic environments and 24 Lionel sets with locomotives journeying across America. Skylines include Dallas, New York, San Francisco, New England, and Washington, D.C., with thousands of figures. Adults $6, Children $3. Proceeds go to Ronald McDonald House of Dallas.

BE STUNNED
BY CHRISTMAS LIGHT DISPLAYS

Highland Park Village is a stunning, colorful wonderland from Thanksgiving to New Year's. Each tree is wrapped in thousands of lights. Just travel a few blocks south of the Village to Armstrong Parkway and tour surrounding blocks in your car, or catch a delightful carriage ride. Highland Park and University Park lights are *bellissimo*!

Interlochen in Arlington is one of the best and largest displays in North Texas. More than 200 homeowners adorn their houses and lawns with assorted themed displays beginning two weeks before Christmas. Allow several hours for a drive-through, 7 to 10 p.m.

Christmas at Frisco Square draws nearly half a million visitors during the holiday months. This is the largest choreographed light and music display in Texas and includes family-oriented activities.

Highland Park Village: Preston Rd. and Mockingbird
Interlochen: Randol Mill Rd. and Westwood Dr., Arlington
Frisco Square: Main St., Frisco

EAT, SHOP, & STROLL
AT THE KNOX HENDERSON DISTRICT

You simply must schedule a full day and evening to stroll the lively Knox Henderson District. It's booming with hotspots, cutting-edge boutiques, charming antique stores, wine bars, pubs, and nightlife galore.

Walk the Katy Trail or enjoy a cup of tea and homemade pastry at Timothy Oulton Dallas. It's the British designer's first stand-alone store in the United States showcasing his English vintage furnishings and treasures. You'll be singing "we all live in a yellow submarine" when you gawk at the nine-foot yellow submarine immersed in the 2,000-gallon fish tank. Let Lisa Garza dazzle you with her charm and fried chicken at Sissy's Southern Kitchen & Bar. Victor Tango's is a must for a craft beer such as the Lakewood Temptress or a Shared Plate with your significant other. With over 1,000 parking spaces, you can park yourself or hail the valet at one of the district's many restaurants.

Timothy Oulton
4500 N. Central Expressway, Dallas, 214-613-2464
www.timothyoulton.com

Sissy's Southern Kitchen & Bar
2929 N. Henderson Ave., 214-827-9900
www.sissyssouthernkitchen.com

Tei Tei Robata Bar
2906 N. Henderson Ave., Dallas, 214-828-2400
www.teiteirobatabar.com

Veritas Wine Bar
2323 N. Henderson Ave., Dallas 214-841-9463
www.veritaswinedallas.com

Victor Tango's
3001 N. Henderson Ave., Dallas, 214-252-8595
www.victortangos.com

Barcadia has vintage arcade games that you haven't seen in years: Donkey Kong to Skee-ball to a giant Jenga set, with about fifteen game selections in all. If you think Dave & Buster's is just too big and busy, then this could be your new cool place. They have killer bar food and 24 beers on tap. Their huge patio is dog-friendly. It's a great place to watch your team win a game. Valet parking is always an added plus.
1917 N. Henderson, Dallas, 214-821-7300
www.barcadiabars.com

GIDDY UP
AT THE RODEO

"This ain't my first rodeo." Can you say that? If not, check out the Mesquite ProRodeo Series, which runs June through August in air-conditioned comfort! President Ronald Reagan, President George W. Bush, and Prince Rainier III have attended the Mesquite ProRodeo. The Texas Stampede Rodeo, at the Allen Event Center, is a first-class event in November and benefits Children's Charities. There are three performances with all sorts of competitions. Of course, there's also the famous Stockyards Championship Rodeo in Fort Worth held in October. It hosts the Red Steagall Cowboy Gathering and the Hall of Fame Rodeo. Who doesn't love a genuine cowboy who just happens to be a super athlete?

Mesquite Pro Rodeo: 1818 Rodeo Dr., Mesquite • 972-285-8777
www.mesquiterodeo.com

Texas Stampede: 200 E. Stacy Rd., #1350, Allen • www.texasstampede.org

Stockyards Rodeo: 121 E. Exchange Ave., Fort Worth • 1-888-COWTOWN
www.stockyardsrodeo.com

VISIT A HAVEN FOR SEA LIFE
AT THE DALLAS WORLD AQUARIUM

Maybe you were not expecting to see so many animals at a home for fish. In this long winding walk with waterfalls, you'll see monkeys, turtles, manatees, penguins, sloths, anteaters, crocs, jaguars, sea turtles, jellyfish, and countless exotic birds. Walk through a 400,000-gallon glass exhibit filled with sharks, rays, and sea turtles. The Mayan exhibit is eight stories tall. Imagine having lunch in this exotic environment. Very enjoyable.

1801 N. Griffin St., Dallas • 214-720-2224 • www.dwazoo.com

Tip:

While in this district, don't miss the Holocaust Museum and "learn about the past in order to impact the future." A group of local survivors created the Center for Education and Tolerance in 2005 in the historic West End District. A larger facility is expected to be built nearby.

211 N. Record St., Dallas, 214-741-7500
www.dallasholocaustmuseum.org

PLAY AND EXPLORE
IN THE HISTORIC WEST END DISTRICT

This thirty-six-block former warehouse district is steeped in history, with buildings dating back to the early 1870s, and is known for its nightlife. The House of Blues has lots of appeal with its spicy food and concerts. Try the laid back atmosphere of the West Inn Pub, pleasing customers for twenty-five years. Catch a Circle G Carriage Ride or a Segway Tour. This is home for Wild Bill's Western Store. For some raucous fun, try Dick's Last Resort, especially for the Gospel Brunch. The district is listed on the U.S. National Register of Historic Places.

START A BUSINESS
IN THE METROPLEX

Tens of thousands of corporations claim Dallas as their hub, making it one of the largest corporate headquarter concentrations in the United States: AT&T Inc., Southwest Airlines, Burlington Northern Santa Fe Corp., Frito Lay, PepsiCo, Match. com, Pier 1 Imports, Friedman & Feiger Attorneys at Law, Energy Transfer Partners, L.P., Texas Instruments, and Alliance Data Systems' Corp. Dallas entrepreneurs of national fame include such names as Ross Perot, Phil Romano, Mary Kay Ash, Jerry Jones, George W. Bush, Roger Staubach, Phil McGraw, Mark Cuban, and Stanley Marcus.

Although Dallas is proud of the corporations and major businessmen that call the Metroplex home, the city is also an ideal place for those just starting on the American Dream of being a small business owner. In 2012, *Fortune* magazine listed DFW No. 2 on the list of business-friendly regions. With a superb business climate, strong support, and a wealth of resources, Dallas allows startups to place their best foot forward. Age separates Dallas entrepreneurs from other cities. While the East and West coasts are dominated by recent MBA graduates, more DFW entrepreneurs have experience on their side.

COMMUNE
WITH SCULPTURES AT THE NASHER

Visitors come from all over the globe to see this world-class collection. It is the last word in famous modern and contemporary sculptures. Raymond and Patsy Nasher began buying the masterpieces in the 1950s. The Nasher Sculpture Garden is a highly esteemed 55,000-square-foot building designed by Renzo Piano. The Garden is a quiet and lovely refuge in the center of skyscrapers. To draw more visitors, there are special seasonal events such as the free "til Midnight at the Nasher," which highlights bands, films, picnic dining, and food available by Wolfgang Puck. You can dine al fresco at One Arts Plaza. Bring your kids, quilts, and lawn chairs.

2001 Flora St., Dallas • 214-242-5100 • www.nashersculpturecenter.org

SCREAM FOR THE HOME TEAM
AT AMERICAN AIRLINES CENTER

The main sports tenants at American Airlines Center (AAC) are the Dallas Stars and Dallas Mavericks. The 21,000-seat arena—near a gaggle of high-rise condos, office buildings, and the swanky W Hotel—is bustling with activity from early October through at least mid-April when the professional sports teams are in season. The Stars new owner Tom Gaglardi's infusion of cash has helped the roster. The Dallas Mavericks claimed the National Basketball Association title in 2011. The Mavericks' Dirk Nowitzki, a perennial All-Star forward, is still worth the price of admission. Like the Stars, the Mavericks sometimes sell out for the better teams, so always check first.

2500 Victory Ave., Dallas
Mavericks: 214-747-6287 ● www.nba.com/mavericks
Stars: 214-467-8277 ● www.stars.nhl.com

Tip:

Victory (Tavern/City Grille), which the Stars and Mavs need more of, is located next to the arena and is a great place for dinner or lunch. Cheaper sports grub is offered at Shooters, which serves a mean taco. It's located directly across from the main entrance to American Airlines Center in the AT&T Victory Plaza.

SEE BRONZE
AT PIONEER PLAZA AND
WILLIAMS SQUARE

In Pioneer Plaza, near the Dallas Convention Center, see three larger-than-life bronze trail rider sculptures herding cattle. All appear to be coming down a hill and crossing a stream. The sculptures cost $9 million, and they commemorate a nineteenth-century cattle drive on the Shawnee Trail, prior to the Chisholm Trail.

The Mustangs of Las Colinas are found at Williams Square at the Las Colinas Urban Center. There is a museum housing other works by the sculptor. Both of these great Western monuments claim to be the largest of their kind in the world.

Pioneer Plaza: S. Griffin St. & Young St., Dallas
Mustangs of Las Colinas: 5205 N. O'Connor Dr., Irving
www.mustangsoflascolinas.com

INDULGE
IN RESTAURANTS WITH A VIEW

Dallas is home to hundreds of high-rises. The tallest is the seventy-two-story Bank of America Plaza, which is also the third tallest building in Texas. You can see Dallas is a progressive culinary mecca when world-famous Wolfgang Puck comes to town! He selected a landmark, the Reunion Ball & Reunion Tower, to house his Five Sixty Asian restaurant. The restaurant sits 560-feet above ground with floor-to-ceiling windows offering 360-degree views as the glowing ball rotates. SER Steak, on the twenty-seventh floor of the Hilton Anatole Hotel, also has floor-to-ceiling windows offering stunning views at night while you enjoy a forty-five-day aged prime ribeye.

Five Sixty by Wolfgang Puck: 300 Reunion Blvd. E., Dallas
214-741-5560 • www.wolfgangpuck.com

SER Steak: Hilton Anatole Hotel: 2201 N. Stemmons Freeway
Dallas • 214-761-7470 • www.ser.com

GLORY IN THE BEAUTY
OF THE FORT WORTH BOTANIC GARDEN

Become Zen-like at this "sanctuary for the senses." The 110 gorgeous acres and numerous small gardens are not far from downtown Fort Worth. Strolling through the gardens is free except for the Japanese Area and the Conservatory. This means you have total access to ten areas totally gratis. It dates back to 1931 and is the oldest botanic garden in Texas. There is a restaurant and all sorts of programs, especially in the summertime. Check schedules for concerts, classes, a fall plant sale, and art displays.

3220 Botanic Garden Blvd., Fort Worth • 817-871-7686 • www.fwbg.org

EXPERIENCE TIME TRAVEL
AT HERITAGE VILLAGE

There is a little ol' nineteenth-century town in the middle of big ol' Dallas. Visit pioneer and Victorian homes and commercial buildings, which were discovered around Texas and reassembled for the Village. See what life was like for ordinary Texans over one hundred years ago. Everyone likes the Sullivan House and the bank. There is no need for a guided tour. There are special events and learning experiences. This is a well-kept secret near the Farmer's Market. Closed during August.

1515 S. Harwood St., Dallas • 214-413-3679
www.dallasheritagevillage.org

ENJOY THE ABUNDANCE
OF DIVERSIONS IN GRAPEVINE

In the 1970s, Grapevine began contributing to the Texas wine industry, but its grapes are not the only thing keeping it on the map today. The historic Towne Center and festivals draw lots of folks year-round. There are almost too many choices: Aquarium, Legoland, Discovery Center, Dinner Theater, sail boat tours on Lake Grapevine, wine tours, antique shops, Grapevine Opry, botanical gardens, Grapevine Mills, Farmer's Market, Lake Grapevine cruises, Golf Galaxy. There are staged train robberies on the vintage railroad. Your ticket buys you a roundtrip ticket in a 1920s or 1930s Victorian coach to the Fort Worth Stockyards. Grapevine is a winner with kiddos.

Visitor Center: 636 S. Main St. ● 817-410-3557
www.grapevinetexasusa.com

GrapeFest: Where purple feet are stylish.
Haven't you always wanted to stomp grapes like Lucy and Ethel? This is a teamwork contest and tons of fun. GrapeFest, held each September for four days in downtown Grapevine, is the largest wine festival in the Southwest. Celebrate the fruit of the vine, new varietals, and People's Choice Wine Tasting. There are five stages of entertainment, a Culinary Pavilion, and a Champagne Terrace.

BE PATRIOTIC
AT KABOOM TOWN

Each July 3, from 5 p.m. to midnight, there is a "happening" ... a nationally known fireworks show in Addison. This explosive party helped put the town on the map as one of the most spectacular Fourth of July festivals in the Southwest. Ground zero is Addison Circle, complete with air show, food, and a dazzling 30-minute fireworks show choreographed to music. Many of Addison's 170 restaurants have viewing parties. Hard-core fans can spend the night at one of the 22 hotels by booking a special package. *Forbes* and AOL rated the Addison show "one of the top ones in the country."

www.addisontexas.net/events/kaboomtown

SEE BILLIONS
AT THE BUREAU OF ENGRAVING

The Bureau of Printing and Engraving in Fort Worth is literally a money factory! You will see the various steps of currency production that lead to wallet-ready bills. Invitations for The White House are also printed at the second such facility outside of Washington, D.C. Expect a security screening and metal detectors upon entering. The admission and parking are free. Open Tuesday through Friday.

9000 Blue Mound Rd., Fort Worth • 866-865-1194
www.moneyfactory.gov/tours

FREE YOUR INNER CHILD
AT SIX FLAGS OVER TEXAS

As amusement parks go, Six Flags still reigns as the "Thrill Capital of Texas." The "six flags theme" is strictly about Texas, but there are about fifteen Six Flags parks around the country. The Arlington amusement park has one hundred rides, live shows, and attractions. The mega-coasters are the Titan and the Texas Giant. The Texas Screamer is a record-breaking 400-foot straight-up ride with a dizzying view. Plus the top-rated Mr. Freeze: Reverse Blast. Lots to scream about. There are combo passes that allow entrance to Hurricane Harbor, the water park with great slides and a lazy river, right across I-30. Wear flip-flops at the water park; bare feet will burn, ouch.

W. Pioneer Pkwy., Arlington • 817-640-8900 • www.sixflags.com

Tip:

White Rock Lake Trails has direct access to the Park Lane Equestrian Center. This is an impressive equestrian park that offers lessons for students of all ages in hunter/jumper/western and dressage. There are three covered arenas. It is on 300 acres and has 150 stalls, making it the largest of its kind in North Texas.

8787 Park Lane, Dallas, 214-221-9777
www.parklaneequestrian.com

PADDLE BOARD
AT WHITE ROCK LAKE PARK

Listen up outdoor fitness fanatics. Besides the jogging and biking trails at White Rock Lake you can perfect your paddle boarding skills. Rent a board by the hour at White Rock Paddle Company. It's not as difficult as it looks. The 1,000-acre White Rock Lake has almost ten miles of hiking and bike trails. There are nineteen kinds of fish and all sorts of wildlife. It's an Audubon Society–designated bird-watching area with picnics, fishing, sailing, a dog park, and more. There have been vast improvements over the years due to concerned citizens and grassroots movements. Welcome to an urban oasis. White Rock is "the best dam lake in Texas." Pun intended.

521 E. Lawther Dr., Dallas • 214-670-4100 • www.dallasparks.org

FIND A FAMILY FEUD
AT SOUTHFORK RANCH

RIP Larry Hagman, who passed away in 2013. The Ewing ranch headquarters and surrounding 300 acres are legendary. Even if you're not a *Dallas* series buff, your visit to the Dallas area might not be complete without a trip out to Parker. Trams take you all over the grounds and you can eat at Miss Ellie's. An evening chuck wagon experience is offered to groups of twenty or more. The house and pool are much smaller than they appeared on television; that's camera magic for you.

3700 Hogge Dr., Parker • 972-442-7800 • www.southfork.com

HAVE A DOGGONE DAY
AT MUTTS CANINE CANTINA

It doesn't get more dog-friendly than this: Mutts' 200-seat beer garden–style patio is a fun place to take your pooch. There are two doggie parks to choose from under large oak trees; one for large and one for smaller types. Humans can enter the parks, but most prefer to chill, eat, or drink on the patio. The staff does the poop-scooping for you. You and your furry friend wear matching tags. There are optional memberships, a small fee for dogs, reasonably priced hamburgers, hot dogs, and a limited breakfast menu. Mutts is an unpretentious outing for doggie parents and friends.

2889 Cityplace West Blvd., Dallas • 214-377-8723
www.muttscantina.com

BE BOWLED OVER
AT THE INTERNATIONAL BOWLING MUSEUM AND HALL OF FAME

St. Louis's loss was Arlington's gain. Formerly situated in the shadows of Busch Stadium in St. Louis, the Museum and Hall were relocated near Rangers Stadium in 2008. The 18,000-square-foot structure is readily recognizable because of the large bowling pin in front of the building. Inside, there are five major areas of interactive exhibits: the Inventors, the Advocates, the Champions, the Innovators, and the Future. Computer kiosks tell the stories of all the Bowling Hall of Famers. Three of the best bowling centers in Dallas are Bowlounge, Bowl and Barrel, and 300 Dallas.

621 Six Flags Dr., Arlington • 817-385-8215 • www.bowlingmuseum.com

HANG WITH THE COOL KIDS
AT GREAT WOLF LODGE

It's a frolicking fun resort for kids! A hotel water park. . . . Now that is what we call unbeatable for family vacays. Besides temperature-controlled water slides and rides, there are adult and kid spas, a large outdoor pool, a kid camp, and special themed bunk beds in the guest rooms. Kids receive a wand to battle the dragon in MagiQuest. There is a nightly fireside story time as a nice way to end the day. Water park passes are included in your stay.

100 Great Wolf Dr., Grapevine • 817-488-6510
www.greatwolf.com

ADMIRE MASTERPIECES
AT THE DALLAS MUSEUM OF ART

This cultural institution, in the heart of the Arts District, rivals the art museums in New York, Washington, D.C., and European cities. The DMA promotes and displays works from every continent over the last 5,000 years in its nine curatorial departments. The museum is free, but there is a charge for special exhibits. The museum is open until midnight on the third Friday of each month. On Thursdays from 6 to 8 p.m., enjoy drinks and live music in the Atrium, where incredible Chihuly glass sculptures beautifully frame an enormous window.

1717 N. Harwood St., Dallas • 214-922-1200
www.dallasmuseumofart.org

TALK TO THE 7,000 ANIMALS
AT THE FORT WORTH ZOO

This don't-miss attraction ranks among the top five zoos nationally. The grounds are manicured with plenty of shade, plant life, and benches. The Fort Worth zoo had a grand reopening in 1992, and over the years various new themed areas have been added. But you came for the animals, right? Two baby elephants have been born here recently. Komodo dragons, meerkats, sloths, and silver back gorillas are also in residence. Zookeepers give talks during a period called Wild Encounters. The Fort Worth Zoo just keeps getting better. Adult tickets are $12, children $9. Wednesdays are half price. Fast food is available, or pack a small lunch. Hand sanitizer is not a bad idea.

1989 Colonial Parkway, Fort Worth • 817-759-7350
www.fortworthzoo.org

It's a family tradition for over 50 years. The Forest Park Miniature Railroad is a five-mile, 40-minute ride round trip. You cross six bridges through the woods, over trestles, to the duck pond and back. Two trains run simultaneously on busiest days. There are two depots for refreshments. Adults $4, Children $3.50

WHISTLE "DIXIE"
AT THE TEXAS CIVIL WAR MUSEUM

Fort Worth, "Where the West Begins," is also home to the Texas Civil War Museum. Three galleries are highlighted: the war collection, the Victorian dress collection, and the United Daughters of the Confederacy Texas collection. A theater hosts the video, "Our Homes Our Rights–Texas in the Civil War." See items owned by generals, and hear the backstories of soldiers alongside their weapons and uniforms. Lots of photos and memorabilia beautifully exhibited. An expansion is in the works. A bargain at $6; open Tuesday through Saturday.

760 N. Jim Wright Freeway, Fort Worth • 817-246-2323
www.texascivilwarmuseum.com

BE UPLIFTED
AT THE MUSIC HALL AT FAIR PARK

The Dallas Summer Musicals (DSM) are the preeminent presenter of Broadway Theater in North Texas. Starting with an opera in 1941, this program has risen to new heights each year with bigger and better productions. The Music Hall has always been a huge asset to Dallas and now even more so, thanks to Executive Director and CEO Michael Jenkins. The spacious, elegant building, which has been refurbished, is Spanish Baroque capped with domes. Wine, beer, and ample restrooms are provided for intermissions. Parking is easy and breezy even if you don't use valet.

909 First Ave., Dallas • 214-565-1116 • www.dallassummermusicals.org

IMPROVE YOUR GAME
AT THE HANK HANEY
GOLF TRAINING CENTER

Haney and his PGA-certified, professional instructors offer "inside year-round, weather-protected teaching," and "state-of-the-art swing analysis on-line," according to their profile. Among the center's features are a natural-turf driving range, chipping/pitching greens, sand bunkers, and putting greens. There also is full-club production, a repair shop, and a full-swing golf simulator. Individual and group lessons, clinics, and even lessons on local courses are offered.

Market Center: 2300 N. Stemmons Freeway ● 214-520-7275
www.hankhaney.com

RUN AWAY
TO THE GAYLORD TEXAN FOR
THE ULTIMATE ESCAPE

Now owned by the excellent Marriott Corporation, this is so much more than just a place to spend the night! The signature glass atrium boasts magnificent lush indoor gardens, waterfalls, activities, and a huge spa. Some suite balconies overlook the enormous atrium where a 72-degree temperature is constantly maintained. The Glass Cactus, located at the edge of Lake Grapevine, is a 39,000-square-foot nightclub that offers live music. Restaurant choices are the Old Hickory Steakhouse, River Walk Cantina, Texas Station Sports Bar, and Zeppole. The water park, Paradise Springs, has a lazy river, and who doesn't love that sort of relaxation?

1501 Gaylord Trail, Grapevine • 817-778-1000 • www.gaylordtexan.com

TWIRL A STOOL
AT HIGHLAND PARK OLD-FASHIONED SODA FOUNTAIN

Sit at the counter on one of the nineteen bar stools and get a healthy dose of nostalgia at the century-plus-old Highland Park Pharmacy. Kids love twirling those stools. Tables are available for larger parties. There is just something about those yummy grilled cheese sandwiches! And no one can leave without ordering a milk shake, sundae, or an extra fizzy phosphate soda. The owners are Gretchen and Sonny Williams, who once owned Minyard's Grocery Stores.

3229 Knox St., Dallas • 214-521-2126
www.highlandparksodafountain.com

KICK SOME TIRES
AT TWO CLASSIC CAR SHOWS

Kids of all ages love car shows. See hot rods, classics, customs, trucks, and vendor exhibits at DFW's two best shows. Check out the pristine, lovingly restored vintage cars at Goodguys Car Show, which is held at Texas Motor Speedway each March celebrating thirty years of automotive festivals.

The Yellow Rose Classic Car Show is held at Will Rogers Memorial Center in Fort Worth every August. It's produced by the North Texas Mustang Club and is one of the largest all-Ford indoor shows in the Southwest.

Goodguys Rod & Custom Association: 925-838-0876
www.good-guys.com

Yellow Rose: North Texas Mustang Club • 817-595-6900
www.yrcs.ntmc.org

Tip:

The Trinity River Audubon Project is the largest civic project in Dallas's history. The redevelopment turns the river's path into the largest urban park in the United States. The 6,000-acre Great Trinity Forest—the largest uncut urban, bottomland hardwood forest in the country—dominates the 10,000-acre park.

INTERFACE
WITH MOTHER EARTH

If you are completely fed up with traffic, noise, and asphalt, and your soul begins to crave the essence of Mother Nature, this is the place to commune with the flora and fauna. Ahh, the countryside. Dallas Nature Center is located on 650 acres with ten miles of hiking trails. The Nature Center features the challenging Fossil Valley Trail, along with eight other hikes of varying difficulty. About 80,000 people a year visit the Nature Center for aquatic tours, insect safaris, fossil excavations, and guided hikes. Trinity River Audubon Center (TRAC) is the place to hire a guide for a float trip, bird-watching, or two-wheeling. TRAC is located in the largest urban hardwood forest in the country. Over the river and through the woods, indeed.

7171 Mountain Creek Parkway, Dallas • 972-296-1955
www.dallasnaturecenter.org

6500 Great Trinity Forest Way, Dallas • 214-309-5812
www.trinityriveraudubon.org

ENJOY THE BEAUTY AND TRANQUILITY
OF LEE PARK

Bordering "beyooootiful" Turtle Creek is a one of a kind place, Lee Park. It is the setting for the totally restored Arlington Hall which has been the back drop for numerous memorial events. One such occasion is the annual Easter Pooch Parade. The grounds are immaculately maintained, which is fitting for the elegant Arlington Hall Conservancy. Lee Park is the perfect picnic spot or starting place for a jog along the creek.

See the heroic-sized equestrian statue of Confederate General Robert E. Lee. He is accompanied by his young aide, also on horseback. An interesting fact about the impressive memorial is that President Franklin D. Roosevelt performed the unveiling in 1936, during the Texas Centennial Exposition which was held at Fair Park. (It took eight years to raise the $50,000 to built the famous statue.)

3333 Turtle Creek Blvd., Dallas • 214-520-0977
www.arlingtonhallatleepark.com

FALL ON YOUR BACKSIDE
AT THE GALLERIA'S ICE RINK

There's always something exciting happening at this internationally renowned shopping complex. There are events such as runway fashion shows, pet adoption opportunities, art exhibits, and holiday programs for children. The centerpiece, the mall's sparkling ice rink, set among the restaurants and shops, has long been a customer favorite. You will find scores of high-end and mid-range stores, from Tommy Bahama, Williams-Sonoma, Louis Vuitton, Gucci, Coach, and Banana Republic. There are thirty-four places for dining, and a Play Place for kids on the third level. The Westin Galleria Dallas is just an elevator ride away, complete with the Oceanaire Seafood Room. The Grill on the Alley and the Grand Lux Café are among the best bets for dining.

Alpha and the Tollway, Dallas • 972-702-7171 • www.galleriadallas.com

COLLECT YOUR THOUGHTS
AT FOUNTAIN PLACE

"The most extraordinary urban space in Dallas," this gigantic, 60-story glass prism is exactly what a contemporary skyscraper should look like. Designed by I. M. Pei, the architectural wonder is said to be the best of his three works in downtown Dallas. The fountain at the base of the building in the plaza is spectacular: 200 water jets, controlled by computers. Avanti Restaurant is the place to dine and enjoy the beauty and mesmerizing effects of the fountains. The building has a tunnel access to the Fairmont Dallas Hotel that is fun to explore.

1445 Ross Ave., Dallas ● 214-855-7766 ● www.fountainplace.com

BE UNCONVENTIONAL
IN DEEP ELLUM

Deep Ellum echoes the blues and jazz from bygone days—nearly a century ago, Elm Street was home to nightclubs, pawnshops, shoeshine parlors, pool halls, and small cafes. Deep Ellum originally served as a new neighborhood for freed slaves after the Civil War. Later, a Ford assembly plant was located here. Today, the area is filled with arts and entertainment venues, tattoo parlors, and hip lofts. The residents who avidly support the area want to "Keep it Weird," like Austin. Local bands play on certain nights in this funky entertainment district. Club Da Da is one of the oldest and most popular venues with three stages. There's an arts festival in Deep Ellum every April.

Commerce, Main, Elm Sts., Dallas • 214-747-3337
www.deepellumtexas.com

PICK THE BEST
AT THE LONE STAR STATE
CLASSIC DOG SHOW

Approximately 2,000 spoiled and pampered canines come to Dallas each July to compete in this event. That equals more than 150 different breeds exhibited for judging. This AKC show is put on by the Texas Kennel Club, Trinity Valley Club, and the Greater Collin County Club. There are lots of vendor booths selling items you never dreamed your pooch would want or need. Admission is $8 for adults and $5 for children. This is a great pastime whether you own a precious furry critter or not.

Dallas Market Hall: 2200 Stemmons Fwy., Dallas • 214-749-5491
www.lonestarstateclassic.com

EDUCATE YOURSELF
AT THE OLD RED COURTHOUSE MUSEUM

The most prominent old building downtown was built in 1892. Citizens must have thought that the $300,000 construction cost was extravagant. Here is a little story about inflation: the cost of just transforming the second floor into a museum was $3.8 million. Learn the complete story of the county with many artifacts housed in four different galleries. The grand old structure sits at a crossroads of activity by the JFK Memorial and Dealey Plaza. It's across the street from the cabin of John Neely Bryan, who is credited with founding Dallas. The Old Red Museum is open 9 to 5 daily.

100 S. Houston St., Dallas • 214-745-1100 • www.oldred.org

VISIT
COMPETITIVE CAMERAS LTD.

Celebrating over three decades in Dallas, Competitive Cameras Ltd. is one of the largest camera stores in the United States. Aficionados travel from all over the world to find the latest digital technology products on the market. This is not just another multimillion-dollar megastore. Growing up working in the camera shop, store owner Eugene Jabbour's greatest talent is explaining the technology and helping you navigate the right product to produce the artistic effect you desire. He teaches you how to use the equipment so no need to read the dreaded manual. It's family-owned and voted No. 1 by Dallas A-List and CBS News. Check out those "must-have" camera bags.

2025 Irving Blvd., Dallas • 214-744-5511 • www.competitivecameras.com

GO GALLERY HOPPING
AT THE DALLAS DESIGN DISTRICT

Everything artsy is happening right here. This area used to be "to the trade only." It is now a blossoming district, mostly open to the public, with retail shops, apartments, lofts, restaurants, a multitude of showrooms, event venues, and lots of hip art galleries. There is a wealth of beautiful furniture, fabrics, and fine art available. You don't have to be a designer to be a consumer. Restaurants in the area: the Meddlesome Moth has forty draft beers, more than eighty-five bottled beer selections, and a nice food menu. Oak Restaurant serves global cuisine and handcrafted cocktails.

Design District, 214-698-1300 • www.dallasdesigndistrict.com

BUDDY UP
WITH A CELEBRITY CHEF

When in Rome, do as the Romans do. When in Dallas and Fort Worth, if you want to be really cool, become best friends with a nationally known chef. You simply must be recognized when you enter a restaurant. Just as actors and actresses are the celebrities in Los Angeles and New York, chefs are truly celebrities in Dallas. You must get to know them. Stalk them if you must. You've seen them on The Food Network, *Iron Chef*, and *Good Morning America* and read about them in *Bon Appetit* and the *New York Times*. Add them to your little black book.

Did You Know?

Several Texas chefs—Stephan Pyles, Dean Fearing, Robert Del Grande, and Anne Lindsey Greer contributed to revolutionary changes in the cuisine of the states of Texas, New Mexico, and Arizona. The Southwestern Cuisine explosion of the 1980s and 1990s changed the way America eats and has expanded its roots to California!

Dean Fearing
Fearing's Restaurant at The Ritz-Carlton
Dallas, 2121 McKinney Ave., Dallas
www.fearingsrestaurant.com

Stephan Pyles Concepts
Samar, Sky Canyon By Stephan Pyles, Stephan Pyles
Restaurant, Stampede 66, multiple locations
www.stephanpyles.com

Jim "Sevy" Severson
Sevy's Grill
8201 Preston Rd., Dallas, 214-265-7389
www.sevys.com

Kent Rathbun
Abacus, Jasper's, Blue Plate Kitchen, multiple
locations
www.kentrathbun.com

Chris Ward
The Mercury
11909 Preston Rd., Dallas, 972-960-7774
www.mcrowd.com

GET INTIMATE
AT A SMALL MUSIC VENUE

Although Austin's music scene gets all the national attention, DFW holds its own. The cozy confines of some of its best venues are a key component to DFW's scene. Most of these bars haven't changed a thing since they opened, and we like it like that. The Grapevine, which is cozy with a crazy atmosphere, has a huge shady patio and attracts all sorts of thirsty patrons. You can snag a fireside picnic table at the fifty-year-old Lee Harvey's. At the Goat, which has the best blues bands and karaoke on Sundays, SMU students mingle with old timers. Adair's has been a great "burgers, beer and live music" bar in Deep Ellum for decades and graffiti adds to the low-country vibe. The Slip Inn is good for dancing. You'll also find some small, funky establishments in Deep Ellum and on Lower Greenville.

Lee Harvey's: 1807 Gould St. • 214-428-1555 • www.leeharveys.com
The Goat: 7248 Gaston Ave. • 214-327-8119 • www.thegoatdallas.com
The Grapevine Bar: 3902 Maple Ave. • 214-522-8466
www.grapevinebar.com
Adairs: 2624 Commerce St. • 214-939-9900 • www.adairssaloon.com
The Slip Inn: 1806 McMillan Ave. • 214-370-5988 • www.theslipinn.com

BECOME A CRITIC
AT A FILM FEST

For forty-four years Dallas has hosted the USA Film Festival and brings the best of Hollywood to our area. Premieres and programs bring thousands to celebrate quality films and to pay tribute to master directors and actors. There are year-round programs such as KidFilm Festival, Academy Awards Night®, Short Film, and Video Competition.

The Dallas International Film Festival (DIFF) also celebrates the spirit of great films. DIFF is an eleven-day event with about 150 films, actor interviews, in-depth panels, awards, and educational programs. Both festivals are held in April.

The Lone Star Film Festival is held at Sundance Square in Fort Worth. The five-day event provides people with their first, and sometimes only, opportunity to see the anticipated films of the year along with interacting with the artists who made them.

www.usafilmfestival.com
www.dallasfilm.org
www.lonestarfilmfestival.com

EXPERIENCE THE FABULOSITY
OF NEIMAN MARCUS

Shop elegantly . . . and lunch exceptionally at the historic, original Neiman Marcus. Lunch at the 1913 downtown store is a Dallas tradition. Try the popovers with strawberry butter at the famous Zodiac Room. Bask in the store's décor and uber-expensive finery of every sort. Visit each floor to see the remarkable array of unique items that were handpicked from all over the world and are featured in the famous Christmas Catalog. In 1969, the company began expanding to other cities. Today, Neiman Marcus comprises more than six million square feet of elegant retail space in the United States and Hawaii. It was sold in 2013 for $6 billion.

1201 Elm St., Dallas • 214-761-2300 • www.neimanmarcus.com

SEEK THRILLS
AT ZERO GRAVITY AND MALIBU SPEED ZONE

Heads up adrenaline junkies! These two amusement parks rate high on the popularity list and are adjacent to one another. Zero Gravity boasts of having the world's only "Thrill Park" with five different extreme rides: Bungee Jump, Nothin' But Net, Texas Blastoff, Skycoaster, and Skyscraper. This isn't for wimps. If you love being thrown in the air and dropped from a five-story crane, this has your name on it. Afterward you can stagger next door to SpeedZone and test your driving skills at Lil Thunder, Thunder Road, Top Eliminator Dragster, Slick Trax, and Turbo Track. SpeedZone also has miniature golf and a video game arcade.

11131 Malibu Dr., Dallas • 972-484-8359 • www.gojump.com

BE PART OF THE MAD FOOLISHNESS
AT THE CEDAR SPRINGS HALLOWEEN STREET PARTY

If you are shock proof and want to see some outlandish and bizarre costumed characters, this is the event for you. Held each year in Oak Lawn the Saturday before Halloween, the Cedar Springs Halloween Party gathers about 10,000 revelers to parade, gawk, and drink libations. This is the biggest and most non-traditional Halloween party in town. You'll want to document some of this festive and foolish behavior by snapping some smart phone photos. Leave the kiddos at home.

Cedar Springs and Oak Lawn, Dallas

SUGGESTED ITINERARIES

FOR THE KIDDOS

GET YOUR SPORTS FIX

FOR MUSIC LOVERS

DATE NIGHT

RETAIL THERAPY

ACTIVITIES
BY SEASON

There's always fun to be had in DFW, but some events and activities are best enjoyed, or only happen, at specific times of year. Below are some ideas to keep you busy no matter the season.

WINTER

Christmas at Frisco Square, 73
Christmas Lights in Highland Park, 73
Cotton Bowl, 36, 61
Interlochen in Arlington Christmas Lights, 73
KidFilm Festival, 119
Lone Star State Classic Dog Show, 112
New Years Eve at Victory Plaza, 20
Trains at NorthPark, 72

SPRING

Deep Ellum Arts Festival, 111
Good Guys Classic Car Show, 105
HP Byron Nelson Golf Classic, 41
Mesquite ProRodeo Series, 76

SUMMER

FALL

INDEX